SPEEDY READS

The True Mystery of
THE MARY
CELESTE

D1353052

Rachel Wright
Illustrated by Pete Smith

■SCHOLASTIC

Scholastic Children's Books,
Commonwealth House, 1-19 New Oxford Street,
London WC1A 1NU, UK

A division of Scholastic Ltd
London ~ New York ~ Toronto ~ Sydney ~ Auckland
Mexico City ~ New Delhi ~ Hong Kong

Published in the UK by Scholastic Ltd, 2001

ISBN 0 439 99256 7

Typeset by Falcon Oast Graphic Art Ltd.
Printed by Cox & Wyman Ltd, Reading, Berks.

*With thanks to David Taylor of the National Maritime Museum for his help
with picture reference on this project.*

2 4 6 8 10 9 7 5 3 1

Contents

Other titles in the *Speedy Reads* series:

Moon Landing by Nick Arnold
Gold Rush by Valerie Wilding
Titanic by Alan MacDonald

Voyage to the centre of attention

Time: *Afternoon of 4th December, 1872: that's four years before the invention of the telephone, 23 years before the invention of radio and 28 years before the first powered flight.*

Place: *The Atlantic Ocean, between the Azores and the coast of Portugal.*

Scene: *A two-masted sailing ship called the* Dei Gratia *is on her way from New York to Gibraltar. Out of the blue, one of her crew spots a similar ship drifting aimlessly. She looks in trouble, but there's no sign of a distress signal. The captain of the* Dei Gratia *gives orders to send a message by flags to the strange ship. (Remember these are the days before phones and radio.) No reply is received. He then orders a small search party to board the ship. They find her to be well-stocked with food and fit to sail, but without a single soul on* board. The name of this silent ship? The Mary Celeste. The cause of her passengers' and crew's disappearance? Nobody knows.

The *Mary Celeste* before disaster struck

Why is the Mary Celeste mystery still making waves?

Shiploads of sailors have disappeared without trace on the high seas; but the vanishing of the *Mary Celeste*'s crew is still remembered because it has inspired great writers and clever hoaxers.

The best-known story based on the mystery was published in 1884. Called "J. Habakuk Jephson's Statement", it told the tale of the *Marie* (not the *Mary*) *Celeste* whose captain and officers were murdered by a sinister passenger and his accomplices. This scary story included very few of the real-life facts of the *Mary Celeste* case. Yet some people took it to be a watertight solution to the mystery. One American newspaper even printed the story as fact. No wonder most of us refer to the *Mary Celeste* as the *Marie Celeste* by mistake!

Since 1884 there has been a tidal wave of books, magazine articles and newspaper stories about the *Mary Celeste*. The most recent novel based on the mystery was published in 1996. That's a staggering 124 years after the deserted ship was found.

SPEEDY TRIVIA

"J. Habakuk Jephson's Statement" was first published anonymously. Later it was found to be an early story

by Arthur Conan Doyle, creator of the famous detective, Sherlock Holmes.

How have hoaxers muscled in on the mystery?

Lots of *Mary Celeste* "survivors" have washed up with the tide – mind you, none of their names can be found on the ship's crew list! But the "survivor" who made the biggest splash was a character called John Pemberton.

In 1926 a magazine article claimed to explain what had really happened to the *Mary Celeste*'s crew. The author of the article said his information came from a Mr Pemberton, who had been the mystery ship's cook. In 1929 the article was turned into a book. The book became a huge hit in the USA and Britain; and before long, a newspaper published an interview with Pemberton including his photograph. By this time, the name John Pemberton was on everyone's lips.

But John Pemberton didn't exist. He was the invention of a hoaxer called L. J. Keating. It was Keating who had written the article, interview and book. And the photograph of Pemberton that appeared in the paper was, in fact, a photo of Keating's dad!

Have any genuine sea-sleuths tried to fathom this ocean mystery?

Indeed they have. And unlike the hoaxers, they have based their solutions on evidence given at the *Mary Celeste* trial. But more about that in the next chapter!

SPEEDY TRIVIA

Legend has it that the Mary Celeste *carried thirteen people – an unlucky number for some. In fact, the ship carried a company of ten. On board were the ship's captain, Benjamin Briggs, his wife, his two-year-old daughter, and seven crewmen. The Briggs' seven-year-old son was left behind with his grandmother. Superstitious sailors thought it unlucky to sail with a woman on board. Yet Mrs Briggs had sailed before, without causing murder, mutiny or any other major mishap!*

The mystery deepens

The captain of the *Dei Gratia*, David Morehouse, wasn't stupid. He knew that a crew who rescued an abandoned ship could claim a reward. This reward is known as salvage. But he wasn't keen to sail the *Mary Celeste* back to shore. The *Dei Gratia* carried only eight men, so he couldn't easily spare the crew to man both ships. Besides, the *Dei Gratia* was carrying an explosive cargo of petroleum and he didn't really want to find himself short of hands in an emergency. So what did he do? Well, he thought about the reward. Then he thought some more. Then he ordered three of his men to patch up the ghost ship and sail her to Gibraltar!

Now, salvaged ships are usually as seaworthy as a sunken sieve. But the *Mary Celeste* was sound enough to sail around the world! Naturally the authorities in Gibraltar wanted to find out why this valuable vessel had been deserted before they handed out a reward. So, within two hours of docking, the *Mary Celeste* was placed under arrest for being an abandoned ship. (Whether she was given the right to remain silent is not known!) And five days later, a court hearing began into the *Dei Gratia's* claim for salvage.

What evidence surfaced at the hearing?

The *Dei Gratia* crewmen who had boarded the *Mary Celeste* in mid-ocean were called to the witness stand. One by one, they were asked to describe conditions on the spooky ship. Here's a speedy account of what they said they noticed:

Evidence: When they discovered the *Mary Celeste*, she was moving slowly at a speed of between one-

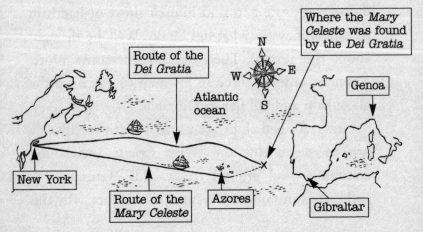

and-a-half and two knots, or nautical miles, an hour. She was more or less on course, but heading *westwards* instead of eastwards.

Comment: *The* Mary Celeste *was due to sail from New York to Genoa, in Italy, via Gibraltar. She left New York eight days before the* Dei Gratia.

Evidence: Two sails were set, one was partly set, one had been run down and was lying on deck, two had blown away, and the rest were rolled up. Parts of the running rigging had blown away; and a long, sturdy rope called the main peak halyard was broken. The severed section of the rope was nowhere to be found.

Comment: *The copper-bottomed hull, masts, spars and standing rigging were all in good nick, and despite the damage to the sails, the ship was still seaworthy.*

When the *Mary Celeste* was found, two of her sails were missing.

13

Evidence: Nearly all the ship's supply of food and drinking water was aboard. The salvage crew who sailed the *Mary Celeste* on to Gibraltar ate the food they found.

Comment: *A salvage crew is a crew who recovers a sunken or abandoned vessel. Legend has it that the salvage crew found a freshly cooked breakfast and mugs of warm tea in the* Mary Celeste*'s galley, or kitchen. This is a load of old barnacles!*

Evidence: Also on board was the ship's cargo of raw alcohol. 1,700 barrels of the stuff. This was the only alcohol found on the ship.

Comment: *Captain Briggs was a deeply religious man who disapproved of drunkenness and never touched anything stronger than tea.*

SPEEDY TRIVIA

In 1872, before refrigerated transport had been invented, food on long distant voyages was often dull. Aboard the Mary Celeste *there was a choice of dried herrings, meat, rice, potatoes, kidney beans, preserved fruits and tinned food, plus flour, nutmeg and sugar for cooking. To drink, there was a choice of tea or water!*

Evidence: There was no sign of damage by fire, smoke or explosion.

Comment: *In those days of wooden ships and paraffin lamps, fire was the hazard sailors dreaded most. When seas were choppy, sailors had to go without hot food because it was too dangerous to light a galley stove.*

Evidence: All the crew's clothes, waterproofs and valuables were on board including their tobacco and pipes.

Comment: *Pipes were prized possessions and no sailor worth his salt would jump ship without his pipe . . . unless he needed to make a speedy exit.*

Evidence: A sounding-rod, used for "sounding" a ship, was found on deck beside the ship's pumps.

Comment: *"Sounding" a ship was done by lowering a sounding-rod into a pump-well to measure how much water had leaked into the ship's bottom, or hold. The sounding rod is usually stored away straight after use. The fact that it was on the deck suggests the missing crew disappeared soon after the water level had been tested. When a* Dei Gratia *crewman "sounded" the ship himself, he found about a metre (three and a half feet) of water in the barrel-filled hold. Not enough to cause alarm.*

Ariel view of deck of The Mary Celeste

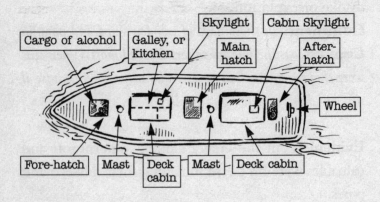

Evidence: The main hatch leading to below deck was closed and barred. The two other hatches at the front and back of the ship were open, and their covers were lying nearby. The fore–hatch led to the cargo of alcohol; the after–hatch led to food stores and spare equipment such as rope.

Comment: *There's no evidence to back-up newspaper reports that the Mary Celeste's hatch covers were found lying upside down. To a superstitious sailor that's a sure sign of bad luck.*

Evidence: There wasn't any sign that the ship had been tipped far over to one side.

Comment: *If she had, her hatch covers would probably have been washed off the main deck.*

Evidence: The tops of the deck cabins were above the main deck. Some of their windows were boarded up.

Comment: *It was usual to board up cabin windows when bad weather threatened.*

Evidence: Water was found sloshing about between decks, and some of the things in the deck cabins were wet. The skylights in the cabins and the galley were open. So too was the outer door leading to the galley.

Comment: *It's possible wind-swept seawater crashed through the open skylights and door. But the glass in the skylights wasn't smashed. The glass paraffin lamps and the spare panes of glass found on board were also intact.*

Evidence: The galley's stove had been knocked out of its chocks, or wedges. All the pots and pans were neatly stowed away. The cargo of alcohol in the hold hadn't shifted. But the barrels of drinking water on the main deck had come loose from their chocks.

Comment: *Whatever moved the heavy cast-iron galley stove out of position must have been mighty forceful. A* Dei Gratia *witness said he thought the stove had been struck by a heavy sea crashing through the open door.*

Evidence: The ship's wheel was unfastened and free. Her compass had been knocked out of place.

Comment: *It takes next to no time to secure a ship's wheel, so this could be a sign that the missing crew left the ship in a mad dash. The compass may have been knocked from its position by someone trying to get at it quickly.*

Evidence: The last entry in the ship's temporary logbook was made on 24th November, 1872. An entry on the log-slate, dated 25th November, 8 a.m., showed the *Mary Celeste*'s last recorded position a few miles off the Azores (near Portugal).

Comment: *A logbook is a book that contains an official record of a ship's voyage. A log-slate is a slate used for jotting down information for the logbook.*

Evidence: The ship's main logbook was missing, along with the ship's papers and two navigational instruments. Also missing was the small lifeboat.

Comment: *Part of the rail surrounding the top deck had been deliberately removed. Could this have been done to help someone launch the lifeboat?*

The mystery deepens.

The unstoppable flood

Few had a clue what to make of the evidence given during the salvage hearing. But Mr Frederick Solly Flood was not one of them. Flood was the Attorney General for Gibraltar. He was also the man who cross-examined the *Dei Gratia* witnesses. As far as he was concerned, something fishy had happened out in the Atlantic. And he was determined to get to the bottom of it. So he ordered an in-depth inspection, or survey, of the *Mary Celeste*. And when the results of this survey didn't satisfy him, he ordered another! Most of the findings Flood and his surveyors made were the same as those reported by the *Dei Gratia's* crew. There were, however, some eye-opening exceptions.

Such as?
Such as these . . .

- One of the ship's rails had what looked like blood stains on it. It also bore the marks of a sharp weapon, possibly an axe.
- Both bows (the front parts of the ship) had cuts in them above the waterline. (In the surveyor's opinion, these cuts had been made recently and deliberately with a sharp instrument.)
- A sword found under the captain's bed looked like it had been covered in blood and afterwards wiped.
- Although seawater was said to have been found sloshing about between decks, the surveyor noted that a rope found under one of the open hatches was bone dry.
- The deck cabins, which were made of thin planks of wood, hadn't suffered the slightest injury. (In the surveyor's opinion, they would have been swept away, or at least cracked, if the deck had been struck by a very violent wave.)
- Items of clothing which the surveyor thought would have got wet had the ship hit very stormy seas showed no signs of any contact with water.
- One of the barrels of raw alcohol looked like it had been tampered with. (Only Flood seems to have noticed this. The surveyor didn't pick up on this in his report.)

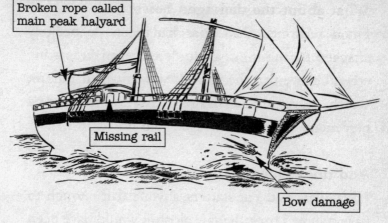

Broken rope called main peak halyard

Missing rail

Bow damage

What was made of these fishy findings?

In a flash, Flood concluded that. . .

1 The blood stains and marks on the rail were evidence of dark doings.
2 The broken barrel was a sign that the crew had had a booze up.
3 The dry rope was proof that the ship had been deliberately drenched in certain places, and not flooded by a wind-swept sea.

As a result, Flood accused the missing crew of murdering Captain Briggs, his family and first mate in a drunken fury, then dumping their dead bodies overboard before fleeing in the lifeboat.

What about the damaged bows?

Flood reckoned that these had been deliberately attacked by the missing murderers to make passing crews believe that the *Mary C* was damaged and not worth salvaging. (Salvage crews were paid a percentage of what a salvaged ship was worth.)

And does Flood's solution hold water?

Like a hair net! For starters, anyone daft enough to have swigged back the raw alcohol would have been horribly sick long before getting drunk. And there were no signs of the struggle you'd expect if a gang of sozzled seamen had set upon their shipmates. Besides, what motive would the *Mary Celeste*'s crew have had for bumping off their captain? Benjamin Briggs was known as a decent, experienced seaman – hardly the sort of chap to drive a crew to mutiny. And there's no reason to suppose his men were a bunch of bullies. In fact, Briggs himself had described them as a "peaceable" lot.

But what about the dry rope, blood stains and bow damage?

The rope proved nothing because it could have been taken from a dry place and put in the open hatch by the salvage crew long after the *Mary C* had been swamped by waves. (Flood forgot to quiz the *Dei Gratia*'s men about that!) The so-called bloodstains were analysed in January 1873 and found to contain no blood at all! And the bow damage may not have been done on purpose. One ship's captain who inspected the *Mary Celeste* in February 1873 reckoned the "cuts" were made by the force of the sea stripping splinters of wood from the hull.

So the mighty Flood's theory was blown out of the water?

Yes, but that didn't dampen his suspicions. He still thought something sinister had happened aboard the *Mary Celeste*. And here's the reason why.

The *Dei Gratia*'s crewmen said they found the *Mary Celeste* on the afternoon of 4th December. That's nine and a bit days after the last date jotted down on her log-slate. By this time she was nearly 400 nautical miles from her last recorded position. Surely it's not possible, argued Flood, for a ship to sail itself for approximately 400 miles and still remain more or less on course?

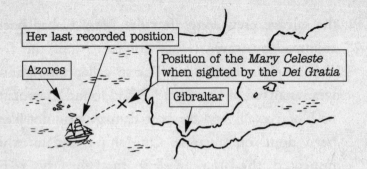

Her last recorded position

Azores

Position of the *Mary Celeste* when sighted by the *Dei Gratia*

Gibraltar

And *is* it possible?

Yes, according to *Mary Celeste* expert and top sea-sleuth, Charles Edey Fay. Check out his sums.

When the *Mary C* was sighted she was going along at between one-and-a-half and two knots. (Remember, knots are nautical miles per hour.) This works out to be 36 to 48 nautical miles a day, or 333 to 444 nautical miles over nine and a bit days. Now, let's suppose that the *Mary Celeste* had more sails set on 25th November than she had when she was found. (Remember, the court heard that some of her sails had blown away.) This would mean that for part of the nine day period she was probably going faster than two knots. In other words, she could have covered more than 444 miles. However, since changing winds must have made her zig-zag a bit, it is possible she could have ended up where she was sighted without a crew to sail her there.

Did Flood ever manage to make a watertight case for murder?

No. But that didn't drown out gossip of deadly doings on board the *Mary C*. One accusation was that the crew of the *Dei Gratia* had murdered the *Mary Celeste*'s passengers and crew in order to claim the salvage reward. Another was that the two captains had planned that Briggs would murder his crew and disappear in the lifeboat, leaving Morehouse to salvage the *Mary C* and split the reward money with Briggs when they met up later.

There was, of course, absolutely no watertight evidence to prove any of this. (For a start, Captain Briggs was part-owner of the *Mary Celeste* and his split of the salvage reward would have been less than his share in the ship.) So, on 14th March, 1873, the court brought the case to a close. The *Mary Celeste* was allowed to continue her voyage to Genoa, with a new skipper and crew; and Captain Morehouse and his men were awarded a salvage payment of £1,700. That was about $8,300 at the time. In the opinion of many sea dogs, this pay-out was mean. Usually salvage crews expected to get about a half or a third of a rescued ship's value. But the *Mary Celeste*, with her cargo, was valued at about $46,000. That means the reward paid out to the *Dei Gratia*'s men was only about a fifth of the money the ghost ship was worth.

Were the missing crewmen kippered by a squid?

Over the years, there have been shiploads of theories to explain the disappearance of the *Mary Celeste*'s crew. Some of these theories have been influenced by the news, trends and interests of their time. And some clearly haven't! Here are just some of the more sensational solutions that have taken the sea-sleuthing world by storm.

Were the missing crewmen kippered by a squid?

The start of the 1900s was a time of great change: modern medicine, electric lights and the petrol engine had recently become part of European life; and the aeroplane had just been invented. So, you might think theories people came up with at this time to explain the *Mary Celeste* mystery would have a scientific or technological ring to them, right?

Wrong! In 1904 a magazine article claimed that the entire ship's company had been abducted by a giant octopus! According to the article, the well–armed creature rose from the deep and grabbed the ship's helmsman. The helmsman's yells brought the rest of the crew up on deck and, one by one, the octopus swept them up.

But could this have been what happened? Well, enormous creatures with terrible grasping tentacles do lurk beneath the waves. Giant squid can be 20m (60 ft) long, with eyes the size of a human head. But if a monster squid is the answer to the riddle, why did all hands remain on deck long enough to be plucked off in turn? And why did the squid make off with the ship's logbook, papers and lifeboat?

SPEEDY TRIVIA

Norse seamen once believed that an octopus-like monster called the Kraken lived in the Norwegian Sea and plucked sailors from their ships. It's now thought that stories of the Kraken may have been inspired by sightings of a giant squid.

Were Captain Briggs and co. carried off into space by a flying saucer?

This theory was first suggested in the 1950s by a UFO investigator called Morris K. Jessup. Unfortunately there is no hard evidence to prove that the *Mary C*'s crewmen were kidnapped by aliens. Nor is it clear why they might have taken their lifeboat into space with them!

SPEEDY TRIVIA

Widespread interest in "flying saucers" took off in 1947, after an unidentifiable glowing object shot across the sky over New Mexico, USA. The day after the sighting, weird wreckage was found under the object's flight-path. Some people say this was the remains of an alien spacecraft.

Did the *Mary Celeste* run aground on the lost land of Atlantis?

Over 2,000 years ago a Greek philosopher called Plato wrote about a mighty land called Atlantis that disappeared beneath the waves. No one has ever been able to find this drowned land; but a medium★

★A person through whom spirits of the dead "speak" to living people.

in the USA reckons it lies along the route taken by the ill-fated *Mary Celeste*. The medium's story goes like this: one day the spirit of Captain Briggs' wife appeared during a seance★ and announced that the lost land of Atlantis had suddenly risen up from the deep, right in front of her husband's ship. Startled, the entire ship's company had stepped ashore; but no sooner had they done so than the land sank, everyone drowned, and the empty ship drifted away.

Strangely enough, it wasn't only the spirit of Mrs Briggs who claimed that Atlantis lay at the bottom of the *Mary Celeste* mystery. In 1926 a journal of astrology suggested that the ship's crew had vanished into thin air while sailing over the sunken land. Apparently this mystical event had been foretold thousands of years earlier . . . by the builders of Egypt's Great Pyramid of Giza!

Were the crewmen swallowed up by the Bermuda Triangle?

Legend has it that there is a sinister area of the Atlantic Ocean that sucks ships, planes and crews to their doom. This deadly zone is known as the Bermuda Triangle. It stretches roughly from

★A meeting set up to try and contact spirits of the dead.

southern Florida to Puerto Rico, up to the island of Bermuda and back to Florida again. Over the centuries many ships and planes have disappeared without trace in the Bermuda Triangle. And one suggestion is that the *Mary Celeste*'s company fell foul of this death-spot, too.

The Bermuda Triangle

But is there really a terrible triangular trap in the Atlantic Ocean? And was the *Mary Celeste* one of its victims? Triangle believers say that the region exerts a powerful force science can't explain (which is a bit of a bummer for those living in Bermuda!). Triangle disbelievers say that this is a load of old bilge water. They reckon the real reason things go missing in the Triangle is because the area is susceptible to sudden storms, savage hurricanes, underwater landslides, giant waves and violent underwater currents.

As for the *Mary Celeste* – she may well have been scuppered by the Triangle's natural or supernatural perils . . . *had she been in the area!* However, since she was well north of the zone, as the route map on page 12 shows, this explanation seems far-fetched.

SPEEDY TRIVIA

Weird goings-on have been reported in the Bermuda Triangle for centuries. But the event that put the Triangle squarely on the map was the disappearance of six aircraft on the same day in December 1945.

Was Captain Briggs two planks short of a deck?
Mental illness can make people do crazy things. And one theory is that Captain Briggs went stark raving mad and murdered his family and crew before flinging himself into the sea. Oddly enough, this suggestion isn't as daft as it sounds. In 1828 a ship's captain did go off his rocker and slaughter his men before chucking himself over the side. (Perhaps the boredom of being cooped up on a small ship with no TV and the same dull dinners was more than he could bear!) But if Captain Briggs did go bonkers,

what became of the ship's lifeboat, papers, missing rope and navigational instruments?

Did the whole ship's company wave goodbye to their senses?

Another theory is that the ship's company was sent crazy by a foul form of food poisoning. Again, this isn't as weird an idea as it seems. In centuries past, before pesticides were used, many people became insane after eating rye, or barley which had been infected with a fungus called ergot. Symptoms of ergot poisoning include seeing imaginary horrors, such as blood pouring down walls, and having fits so violent that sufferers have to be strapped down to stop them injuring themselves. The last epidemic of ergot poisoning took place in France in August 1951. Two hundred people from the same village suffered nightmarish visions and fits after eating infected bread from a local bakery. One elderly villager became so delirious, she threw herself out of a window.

So were the *Mary Celeste*'s passengers and crew driven dotty by ergot poisoning too? The sane answer is . . . probably not. If the food on board the *Mary Celeste* had been dodgy, why hadn't the salvage crew who sailed the ship on to Gibraltar gone mad? After all, we know from the trial that they ate the food they found on board the ghost ship without suffering ill effects.

SPEEDY TRIVIA

From the 15th to the 17th centuries, if someone suffered from fits or visions, it was often thought that they had been "bewitched". An outbreak of bewitchment was usually followed by a witch hunt. And thousands of innocent men, women and children were hanged for witchcraft. Recent research, however, has shown that witch hunts in Europe and the US were linked to rye growing regions. So it seems that ergot poisoning, not witchcraft, was probably to blame for the scary symptoms of bewitchment.

Did plundering pirates kill Captain Briggs and his crew?

Some people have suggested that pirates murdered Captain Briggs, his family and crew. But if pirates were to blame, where were the traces of violence you'd expect to see after a raid? And if sea-robbers had swarmed aboard the *Mary Celeste*, why hadn't they looted the ship from stem to stern? Amongst the things found on board by the salvage crew were a silver watch, a fancy sword, some gold jewellery and expensive clothes.

Were the crewmen scared witless (and shipless) by an iceberg?

It has been suggested that the crewmen abandoned ship to escape from an iceberg coming their way . . . although what an enormous chunk of ice was doing floating about the warm waters of the Azores is anyone's guess.

Riddle in the rigging

Let's suppose for a moment you don't believe in killer squid, self-raising lands and extraterrestrial kidnappers. What hard sea-faring facts are there that might give us a clue as to the likely fate of the missing crew?

Hard sea-faring fact No.1: the ship's lifeboat was missing. This suggests that everyone abandoned ship. An overloaded lifeboat can easily capsize in stormy seas; so the passengers and crew could have drowned.

Hard sea-faring fact No. 2: apart from the lifeboat, only a few practical bits and bobs were missing. This suggests that the crewmen had no time to grab personal possessions and probably abandoned ship in a hurry.

Hard sea-faring fact No. 3: the ship showed no signs of serious damage, by fire, explosion or collision. This suggests that whatever catastrophe the crew feared was about to happen never took place.

But what might that false fright have been?

Did the crewmen fear they were about to be blown to blazes?

Picture this scene. The *Mary Celeste* is on her way from chilly New York to the milder Azores. As she sails through the warmer waters, the temperature in her hold rises. This causes the barrels of alcohol in her hold to leak and give off dangerous fumes. The fumes slowly build up in the sealed hold to create an explosive gas. One morning, a member of the crew opens the fore-hatch, leading to the hold. The smell of the fumes rising up from below hits him, smack bang in the face. Terrified, he alerts his captain. Knowing it would only take a spark to ignite the fumes and blow the ship to smithereens, Captain Briggs yells out the order to abandon ship. The crewmen drop what they are doing and hurry across to the lifeboat. In a mad panic, Captain B grabs the ship's papers and two navigational instruments. Then he jumps into the lifeboat with his family and crew. The small overloaded boat starts to bob away from the ship. But no sooner has it done so than a towering wave crashes over it, sending everyone aboard to a watery grave.

But does this explosion theory fit the known facts?

Check out the following and see:

Fact: When unloaded, the cargo of alcohol was found to be "missing" nine barrels.

This could mean that either. . .
a) Nine of the 1,700 barrels couldn't be found.
b) Nine barrels-worth of alcohol had leaked from the cargo.
c) Nine actual barrels had leaked during the voyage.

Fact: The fore-hatch that led to the cargo of alcohol was found open.

At the court hearing the first mate of the *Dei Gratia* said that his ship had been battered by storms.

Therefore it's likely the *Mary Celeste* had also weathered storms before she was found. We know that the *Dei Gratia* had kept her fore-hatch closed for most of her Atlantic crossing. If the *Mary Celeste's* fore-hatch had also been kept closed for much of her voyage, to stop whopping great waves pouring below deck, the alcohol fumes wouldn't have been able to escape. Now, suppose a member of the crew had opened the hatch early on 25th November, when we know the weather had calmed down. Wouldn't the discovery of fumes have sent everyone scrambling for the lifeboat? After all, it would only have taken one spark to blow a fume-filled ship skyward.

Fact: Water was found sloshing below decks, and some of the sails and rigging were missing.

Wind-driven waves could have crashed over the deck and down the open hatches after the crew had left in the lifeboat. Without the crew to keep her in trim, the *Mary Celeste's* sails and rigging could have been torn down by the wind.

STOP PRESS: *According to the late Captain Henry Appleby, the crew of his ship, the* Daisy Boyton, *took fright* *and began to abandon ship because of a "catastrophe" that never occurred. Here's what happened:*

The *Daisy B* was on her way to Spain when suddenly her hatches blew off and smoke plus a crackling noise rose up from her hold. Thinking the ship was on fire, the crew rushed to the lifeboats. Only Captain Appleby remained calm. Unlike his crew, he knew that the cause of this commotion wasn't fire, but ice! The wooden wedges used to keep the ship's cargo of petrol steady had been loaded in chilly weather and ice had got into the wood. As the ice warmed up on the way to Spain, it crackled and melted and gave off a vapour. And it was this vapour, mixed with the petrol fumes, that had blown the hatches heavenward.

What about the broken rope, the main peak halyard? How does that fit into the picture?

Sea-sleuth and sailor Dr Oliver Cobb reckons the crew used the rope as a tow-line. Their plan? To pull their lifeboat back to the ship if the expected explosion never happened. But this plan was scuppered when a savage wind sprang up and the *Mary C* suddenly surged forwards, breaking the tow-rope and drowning the lifeboat. (Weather reports of the time say that on the morning of 25th November, 1872 the wind was light, but by afternoon it had picked up dramatically.)

Dr C. also reckons that a member of the crew probably opened the after-hatch (that led to spare equipment) in order to get a new rope for the tow-line, then changed his mind and used the main peak halyard rope instead. After all, new rope can take time to uncoil and the main peak halyard was already at hand.

So "fear of explosion" is the answer to the *Mary Celeste* riddle?

It might be . . . but then again, it might not. You see, not everyone is convinced that the leaking barrels of alcohol would have given off gases. One sea-sleuth, Gershom Bradford, says that any leaks would have mixed with the sea water in the bottom of the ship and have been pumped out. (It was usual in wooden ships to pump out the hold every morning.) An alcohol expert adds that even if the alcohol had given off fumes, they would have been invisible. So, how would the crew have known about them? Of course, they might have been alerted by the smell of the fumes. Or perhaps the build-up of fumes caused one of the barrels to blow its top, which would have made a thunderous sound. But we can't *prove* any of this.

Does that leave us all at sea?

Not necessarily. There's another impending disaster that would scare the salt out of any captain and crew. And that's the sinking of their ship.

Down to the bottom of the deep blue sea

Did Captain Briggs and his men believe their ship was going down? Sea-sleuth Gershom Bradford certainly thinks so. His theory is that the *Mary Celeste* was hit by a waterspout:

A waterspout is a small tornado at sea. The pressure at the centre of a 'spout is much lower than outside. This creates a vacuum that sucks things into the air and blows out windows and walls.

Imagine this. The *Mary Celeste* is crossing the Atlantic when suddenly a whirling funnel of wind and water appears out of nowhere and roars right over her. Quick as a flash, the pressure inside her hull drops, and the water in her hold is sucked high up the pump-well. Fast as a wink, her skylights pop off, and wind-driven water crashes through to the decks below. Terrified, the crew dive for cover. And when the sail-ripping, rope-splitting winds die down, one of them "sounds" the ship to see if the hull is leaking. To his horror, he finds bucket-loads of water in the pump-well. Convinced that their ship is sinking faster than a stove, Briggs and his crew launch the lifeboat ... and are never heard from again.

But does this theory fit all the known facts?
Check for yourself:

Fact: *The* Mary Celeste *was discovered in the Atlantic Ocean.*

Waterspouts occur mostly in the tropics. But they can strike just about anywhere. They can also appear over calm seas without warning and disappear in a flash.

Fact: *A dropped sounding-rod suggested that the ship had been "sounded" not long before the missing crew's disappearance.*

Water would have remained high in the pump-well for some time after the 'spout had passed. If the crewman who "sounded" the *Mary C* didn't know this, he would have thought that the ship was sinking.

Fact: *Two hatch covers were open, and water was reported sloshing about below decks.*

A 'spout speeding over the *Mary Celeste* could have caused the hatch covers to blow off and the skylights to pop open. (The walls of buildings explode outward when hit by a tornado and a waterspout would probably have the same effect.) The ship's main hatch may have stayed shut because it was covered by the lifeboat.

Once the hatches and skylights were open, there would have been nothing to stop swirling seawater from flooding below deck.

Fact: *Glass and other breakable objects were found unbroken.*

Like tornadoes, waterspouts often follow a narrow path. They might destroy something directly in their path, but leave safe something only a few metres away. Perhaps this explains why the *Mary C*'s glass paraffin lamps and skylights were found unbroken, and why some of the ship's sails and rigging were undamaged.

Just so you know: Gershom Bradford reckons that the *Mary Celeste*'s sails must have blown away before she was abandoned because it would have been too tricky to launch a loaded lifeboat with five sails set.

SPEEDY TRIVIA

On 26th April, 1991, over 50 tornadoes touched down in Kansas, USA, killing 21 people. One of the dead was sucked out of his car by the storm and thrown into a nearby field. Later, friends found the dead man's seatbelt still fastened in his car. They also found two bottles of whisky in the car's boot — unbroken.

But is a swirling 'spout the solution to this age-old mystery?

The men who surveyed the *Mary Celeste* in Gibraltar said that there was no evidence that she'd been at the heart of a monster storm. But did they know about the weird ways of waterspouts? One of the *Dei Gratia*'s crew said in court that he believed that the *Mary Celeste*'s men had panicked about something. He said that they sounded the ship, "and found perhaps a quantity of water in the pumps at that moment, and thinking she would go down, abandoned her". But no one thought to cross-examine him about his statement.

Could another type of freak phenomenon have done for the *Mary Celeste*'s crew?

One suggestion is that an underwater earthquake erupted beneath the *Mary C*, causing some of the alcohol barrels to leak and panicking the crew into abandoning ship.

Another possibility, suggested by Dr Richard McIver, is that the crewmen were victims of bubbling gas. Check out his reasoning. Under the ocean there are deposits of frozen gas hydrates. In certain conditions these gas hydrates are stable. But rises in temperature and dips in pressure can cause them to "melt". And when that happens, a mega amount of gas bubbles up violently through the water. Now, bubbling sea water is fine if you're a whale in need of a jacuzzi! But if you're on board ship it's a different story. That's because a ferociously bubbling sea can drastically reduce a ship's buoyancy, or "floatability", causing it to sink speedily.

Picture this scenario. The *Mary C* sails over a release of bubbling gas. Immediately she starts to float extremely low in the water. Thinking his vessel is only seconds away from sinking, the captain gives the order to abandon ship. In a dash, the crewmen launch the lifeboat into the bubbling water . . . and it sinks like a stone. Moments later, the bubbling gas breaks through the surface of the water and drifts away into the air. With the gas gone, the *Mary Celeste*'s buoyancy returns, and she sails away over the horizon.

SPEEDY TRIVIA

A chemist called Dr Donald Davidson discovered that released methane gas hydrates can reduce buoyancy. In 1984 he suggested that 'melting' gas hydrates might explain some of the mysterious disappearances in the Bermuda Triangle.

So bubbling sea gas could be the answer to this unfathomable mystery?

Who knows! The maddening truth is, we shall

probably never be able to prove any likely theory as to the *Mary Celeste*'s fate. Too many questions were left unasked at the court hearing for us to answer the riddle. And the clues to the mystery, like its leading characters, are all long gone. Only the sea now knows what really happened on that fateful day in November, 1872 . . . and the sea keeps its secrets well.

One hull of a ship!

There's a lot about the *Mary Celeste* mystery that we will never know. But one thing's for certain. The ship had more bad luck than a turkey at Christmas! She was built in 1860–1, shortly before steamships slowly began to replace sailing ships in fashion. (By the end of the 1800s engine-powered steamships could cover long distances faster than sailing ships. They could also carry more cargo.) At first, the *Mary C* was called *Amazon*. But the start of her career was far from amazing. No sooner had she been launched than she damaged her hull and had to be sent for repairs. Not long out of the shipyards, she collided with another ship and, before you could say "Shiver me timbers", she was back being repaired. Another accident later, her name was changed to *Mary Celeste*. And under this name she drifted from one mishap to another. On one voyage she was badly storm-damaged; on another her cargo of live animals died. And in 1884, she fell into the hands of a fraudster. He loaded her up with a dummy cargo, which he insured for a purse-popping amount. Then he deliberately ran her aground and set her alight in the hope of getting a hefty insurance pay-out.

And did this crime pay?

No. The insurance companies got wind that something dodgy was up, and the arsonist was taken to court. A legal hiccup saved him from the hangman's noose. (Capital punishment was widespread in those days.) But he died in poverty and disgrace.

Did any of the *Mary Celeste*'s captains escape her jinx?

Not so you'd notice. Her first captain died a few days after being put in charge; another was sacked from his job; a third left after a collision with another ship; and, as you know, Captain Briggs disappeared along with his wife, daughter and crew.

Could an entire ship's company vanish into thin air today?

It's unlikely. In the nineteenth century, before radio and faster steamships, the world's main shipping lanes were littered with lost lifeboats and rotting bodies. Nowadays this is no longer the case. We have much faster forms of transport which means far-ranging searches can be carried out speedily by air and sea. We also have a highly sophisticated global communications network. This means ship-to-shore contact can be kept at all times, and Missing Persons details can be sent round the world in a flash. (In 1872 the speediest type of long distance communication was the electric telegraph, which took hours, not minutes, to send messages across the world.)

SPEEDY TRIVIA

Nowadays sailors, pilots and mountaineers keep track of where they are using Global Positioning System (GPS) receivers. Today's adventurers can wear a GPS receiver like a watch and use it to calculate their whereabouts to within a few metres. The GPS network uses 24 satellites that continually circle 17, 700 km (11, 000 miles) above the Earth. Each receiver picks up signals from the satellites which allow it to calculate its user's exact position.

Finding missing crews is clearly easier now than it was back in the 1800s. But that doesn't mean it's always plain sailing. On 28th July, 2000, four people and their yacht went missing in the North Sea. There followed a three-day air and sea search by seven lifeboats, five spotter-planes and a helicopter. Yet neither the crew nor the yacht could be found. A final search by a plane, carrying up-to-the minute technological equipment, also failed to find anything. It wasn't until two weeks later that the missing crew's bodies were spotted in the sea by Dutch fishermen. The yacht is still missing.

Further Information

What do *you* think happened to the *Mary Celeste*? If you want to delve more deeply into the mystery, here are some detailed adult books and web sites you might like to check out. Together with this book, they may help you come up with your own solution to the case. Happy sleuthing!

Adult Books:

- *The Story of the Mary Celeste* by Charles Edey Fay. Published by Dover Publications in 1988.

Probably the most thorough book ever written about the Mary Celeste. Contains plenty of information about Captain Briggs and his crew, plus descriptions given by the witnesses at the Mary C's court hearing.

- *The Secret of the Mary Celeste and other sea fare*
  by Gershom Bradley.
  Published by Barre Publishing in 1966

Explains in detail the waterspout theory.

Internet Addresses:

http://www.deafwhale.com/maryceleste/
index.html
Explains the underwater earthquake theory.

http://scientium.com/editors/mcnamara/
bermyth.htm
Looks at how gas hydrates could be to blame for
some unexplained sea disappearances.

SPEEDY READS

Want to find out the facts, and quick?
Make a mad dash to get some other speedy reads!

Moon Landing
by Nick Arnold
Moon Landing tells the true story and answers
the questions on the most important event in
scientific history.

Gold Rush
by Valerie Wilding
Gold Rush tells the true story and answers all
your questions on the event that changed the
face of America, for ever.

Titanic
by Alan MacDonald
Titanic tells the true story and answers all your
questions on the biggest sea disaster of the
20th century.

**Speedy Reads – no more than you need
to know!**

Dreadful Drama
by Rachel Wright

First ancient Greek guys put on masks and
acted out top tales.
Next Shakespeare and his pals had some huge hits.
Now the world's a stage to all sorts – from plays
with no words to actors with no clothes!

In this behind the scenes guide you'll meet an
actress who slept in a coffin, a playwright who
lost the plot, and a director with all the talent of
a corridor. You'll turn the spotlight on stage
fights, fake props and special effects, and find out
if you've got what it takes to write a smash-hit
play or be a mega stage star.

So lights down for some dreadfully dramatic
action. It's quite a performance.

**If you want to be in the know, get
The Knowledge!**

TOP·TEN

Classics
by Valerie Wilding

What are the greatest stories of all time?
Want to know which classic story has the
number one slot out of hundreds of terrific tales?
It could be...

Around the World in Eighty Days – Quick!
Join the chase as Detective Fix follows Phileas
Fogg and Passepartout to the ends of the earth
and back again.

Black Beauty – come along for the ride of
your life through fires and floods and get the
story straight from the horse's mouth.

Wuthering Heights – Mystery and romance on
the moors with Heathcliff and Cathy – it's wild!
With top ten fact sections, including outrageous
explorers' tales, a travel quide for fantasy islands,
and ten real cut-throat pirates!

**Classic stories as you've never seen
them before.**

TOP·TEN

Dickens Stories
by Valerie Wilding

What was top of the pops in Victorian times?
Want to know which Dickens story's had the
number one slot since the 19th century? It
could be…

Great Expectations – take a peep in Pip's
diary and expect takes of escaped convicts and
romance gone horribly wrong!

A Tale of Two Cities – The French are
revolting and anyone could end up on the gory
guillotine. Can our heroes and heroines keep
their heads?

Oliver Twist – Starved orphan kidnapped by
bad Bill Sikes! Join the manhunt with the
Crimes R Us TV crew.

WITH top ten fact sections, including crime,
punishment, nasty nightmare schools and kids
up chimneys.

**Dickens stories as you've never seen
them before.**